TRUE FAITH

My Emmaus Walk:
A Personal Experience

TRUE FAITH

My Emmaus Walk:
A Personal Experience

Elgie Loyd

TRUE FAITH

My Emmaus Walk: A Personal Experience

ELGIE LOYD

True Faith
My Emmaus Walk: A Personal Experience
Copyright © 2015
Elgie Loyd

Printed in the United States of America

Catalogued in the Library of Congress

ISBN 978-0692409299

Published by
Jabez Books
A Division of Clark's Consultant Group
www.clarksconsultantgroup.com
www.jabezbooks.com

Jabez Books

DEDICATION

This book is dedicated to my entire family: mainly, Van Loyd, Sr., LaTocha Muckleroy, Van Loyd, Jr., and Christopher D. Loyd. I also dedicate it to all of my sisters and brothers in Christ Jesus, with a "Special Thanks" to Rev. Archie C. Browne, and his wife, Eleanor, who have been my "Spiritual Mentors" since I have been at Hamilton Park United Methodist Church. May everything that has breath praise the Lord, and may the love of my heart be of every bright color – a reflection of God's image.

CONTENTS

INTRODUCTION

I believe the inspiration that led to the writing of this book was a divine experience. I love the Lord with all my heart, soul and mind, but I have never considered myself worthy enough to be in His presence in spirit or body. I cannot deny my disobedience and my sins, for they have been many before me.

As a matter of fact, I am in full agreement with Paul when he said in Romans 7:14 "I know that the law is spiritual; but I am unspiritual, sold as a slave to sin. I do not understand what I do. For what I want to do, I do not do; but what I hate, I do. And if I do what I do not want to do, I agree that the law is good. As it is, it is no longer I myself who do it, but it is sin living in me. I know that nothing good lives in me, that is, in my sinful nature. I have the desire to do what is good, but I cannot carry it out. What I do is not the good I want to do; no, the evil I do not want to do – this I keep on doing."

It was not until I through the Spirit (giving Jesus all praise and honor) came to **Believe and Claim** my **Salvation** through **Jesus Christ** that I am now able to write this book and run the race that has been laid out before me from the beginning of my birth. For I know now it is nothing that I have done, nothing that I can do. No amount of money or fame can **Save Me**. It is only through the **Blood of Jesus (by Grace given to me by God)**

that I am Saved, and nothing can disqualify me from the prize.

<u>Claiming Romans 8:35-39</u>

"Who shall separate us from the love of Christ? Shall trouble or hardship or persecution or famine or nakedness or danger or sword?

"As it is written: 'For your sake we face death all day long; we are considered as sheep to be slaughtered.'

"No, in all these things we are more than conquerors through Him who loved us. For I am convinced that neither death nor life, neither angels nor demons, neither the present nor the future, nor any powers, neither height nor depth, nor anything else in all creation, will be able to separate us from the love of God that is in Christ Jesus our Lord.

"Now to Him who is able to do immeasurably more than all I ask or imagine, according to His power that is at work within me, to Him is glory in the Church and in Christ Jesus throughout all generations, forever and ever! Amen."

Chapter One

The Voice

I will never forget it. It was Super Bowl Sunday, January 26, 2003, and my husband, Van, and I had been home from church for about 30 minutes. I was stirring around in the kitchen preparing some snacks and soda with anticipation of watching the Super Bowl game on the big screen TV.

As I opened the refrigerator and reached in to get the meats, cheese and fruits, I heard a "voice" call my name, "Elgie." I rose up and turned around to see if someone was there, but there was no one. I turned to continue what I was doing when I heard it again. "Elgie," the voice repeated softly, but clearly. I looked around the room again, but I saw no one. I then went down the hall to the bedroom to ask Van if he was calling me (for I was so sure I had heard someone), but as I opened the door and answered, "What?" he spoke back with confusion, "I didn't call you."

"You didn't call my name?"

"No."

"I thought I heard you call me twice."

"Well, I didn't. Maybe its old age; they say your hearing is the first to go," as he started to joke and laugh.

"Yeah, right," I laughed, closing the door to walk back to the kitchen. But I was still puzzled. I just knew I heard someone call my name, but Van and I were the only ones in the house.

I went back to the kitchen and continued preparing the snacks.

The Cowboys were not playing, so my focus was starting to turn toward the food and some quality "football time" with my husband. As I reached for a tray to put the meat on, I heard that same voice call my name a third time.

"Elgie."

It said, "Elgie, I want you to take your Emmaus Walk on the first walk after the Prayer Summit." I then turned around very quickly, for I knew the word Emmaus was relating to something spiritual, and the Prayer Summit was a powerful prayer service being held on March 28th, 29th and 30th at our church, Hamilton Park United Methodist. The Prayer Summit will feature the powerful guest speaker, Pastor Suzette Caldwell of the Kingdom Builder's Prayer Institute in Houston, Texas. The service would be hosted by our church's intercessory prayer team, which I am a member. So I knew if Jesus wanted to do anything with or through me (change me, restore me, heal me, fill me, make me over, etc.), He could do it at the Prayer Summit. So I stopped to listen to the voice, but quickly reminded myself at that point that surely I must be losing my mind. God is not talking to me.

Nevertheless, I began to listen very closely, then I heard it again, "Elgie, I want you to take your Emmaus Walk on the first walk after the Prayer Summit." And before I knew it, I was communicating with the Spirit in my mind.

> *"The Spirit just spoke to me and said now would be a good time for Elgie to take her Emmaus Walk."*

"Lord," I said, "Do You want me to take my Emmaus Walk after the Prayer Summit?" As I ask the question, I'm thinking to myself that surely I'm not worthy.

"Yes, I do," the voice spoke back.

I became nervous and started to sweat, this seemed all too real. I was getting scared because I started to remember what happened just a few months ago at an intercessory prayer meeting. We were breaking up to go home when Michael turned to Beverly (two of my intercessory prayer partners) and made the statement, "The Spirit just spoke to me and said now would be a good time for Elgie to take her Emmaus Walk."

We all looked at each other and started laughing. But Michael continued, "No, I'm serious. The Spirit says this would be a good time for you, Elgie. Now, while you are still off from work (I was unemployed at the time), think about it," he said, walking away.

I did believe Michael was serious, and it made me feel good to hear that he and Beverly had faith and belief in the Spirit of God in me.

For a long time I had known Michael and Beverly through my membership at Hamilton Park, and I believe with all my heart that Michael is a "Man of God" and Beverly is a "Woman of God." So for the two of them to have been in agreement with the Spirit, I received it with great joy!

But now, standing here in my kitchen, I was getting scared. The voice I kept hearing seemed too real, and I felt like I was not ready.

However, I thought to myself, "I know! I got it! If this is from the Spirit of the Lord, God Almighty, then He already knows (unlike Michael and Beverly) that I don't really even know what an Emmaus Walk is." So, I continued to prepare the food for the Super Bowl game and to communicate with the Spirit in my mind.

I responded (in the spirit), "Lord, You must know that I don't even know what an Emmaus Walk is," thinking I was getting off the hook.

"I know that. But you said if I would send you that you would go. Now, do you not want to go?"

Sweat popped out of my body, and I was feeling like my back was up against the wall. I have never felt such closeness to the Lord, but I still wasn't sure if He was talking to me about this situation or if I was deceiving myself, but I continued communicating anyway.

"I do want to go, Lord, but I don't know what to do or how I would go about taking an Emmaus Walk. What is the Walk? Where is the Walk?"

These questions filled my head with a great rush and I became overwhelmed. I began to think that I was fooling myself and that God would never directly come to me, let alone ask me to go anywhere. So I tried to push this whole experience "under the rug" for that moment.

I could still hear the Spirit asking me, "Do you understand what I want you to do?" Because I am a believer in the Word and trust the Spirit of God, I could not just ignore this message or pretend that it wasn't happening.

I finished getting the food together, then I grabbed the soda that was chilling in the freezer, but as I was leaving the kitchen, the Spirit of God would not leave my mind and let me focus on the upcoming game.

I could still hear the Spirit asking me, "Do you understand what I want you to do?" Because I am a believer in the Word and trust the Spirit of God, I could not just ignore this message or pretend that it wasn't happening. I heard the voice speaking to me, and it called me by name. Yes, it sounds crazy, that's what I thought, too. But I was too afraid of what could happen to me if I didn't heed the message versus what would happen if I followed through. So, just in case it was "real" and the fact that this whole experience caused a burning in my heart as I stood there, I decided to call someone.

Ring, Ring.

"Hello, Beverly, this is Elgie. I'm sorry to bother you on this Super Bowl Sunday."

"Hey, girl, you're no-bother, what's up?"

"Beverly, for some reason I feel the Spirit is speaking to me about my Emmaus Walk, telling me that I should take my Walk right after the Prayer Summit. But, I don't know if it's the Spirit speaking to me or if it's just me. So I wanted to tell someone because I'm over here trying to "sweep it under the rug," and if it turns out to be the Spirit, I'll need someone to help me stay accountable. Will you please help me?"

"Sure, I'll help you."

"Oh, thank you, because Beverly, to be honest, I don't even know what an Emmaus Walk is."

"That's okay, girl. Do you have access to the internet?"

"Yes."

"Good, then write down this address and pull it up on the internet. There's some information that you need to read and sign. Check the dates for the next Walk, and print out the form. Read over it and bring it with you on Wednesday to the Booster Service so we can present it to Rev. Wright and Rev. Lee. I'll be in prayer with you until then."

"Oh, thank you, Beverly. I'll read it and see what I have to do."

"Very good...call me anytime, I don't mind."

"Thanks, have a good day and enjoy the game."

"Okay, bye-bye."

As I hung up the phone with Beverly, my spirit immediately felt calm, and I was glad that she was there for me. At first, I was a little disappointed, because I was hoping she would do all the legwork. But the Spirit knew that I was lazy, and even Beverly knew there was information I would need to know and remember, so I was grateful to do the research.

REFLECTIONS

_____

_____

_____

_____

_____

_____

_____

_____

_____

_____

_____

_____

_____

_____

_____

_____

_____

_____

Chapter Two

Provision

Within the next day or so, I had retrieved the Emmaus Walk information from the internet and started to read it. I had learned that the next Walk was Walk #168, scheduled for Thursday, April 24th at 7pm through Sunday, April 27th at 7pm. It was being held at one of the local Encampments in Dallas, Texas, and all the forms and information explaining the process and procedures were there on the internet to read. I would need a sponsor, and there was a small fee. I vaguely remember

Beverly mentioning something about that, but she said not to worry, because that would be taken care of once the Church had viewed my form for approval.

That's one thing I can say about myself. I don't depend on anyone else to search the scriptures for me; I do that for myself. I may not always understand in full detail all that I read, but I do read for my own knowledge and revelation, and in doing so, beyond my amazement.

Well, I kept reading, and to my surprise, there it was, the scriptures showing me where to find the story in the Bible explaining the Emmaus Walk (Luke 24:13-35). In those scriptures I found the answer to the question that had been weighing on my mind for over two days: What is the Emmaus Walk?

The walk to Emmaus is a spiritual renewal program intended to strengthen the local church through the development of Christian disciples and leaders. My Spirit immediately became excited, and I rushed to my private place to retrieve my Bible and read the story in Luke of the walk on the road to Emmaus.

That's one thing I can say about myself. I don't depend on anyone else to search the scriptures for me; I do that for myself. I may not always understand in full detail all that I read, but I do read for my own knowledge and revelation, and in doing so, beyond my amazement, I receive joy and strength every time I encounter the Word of God. One of the main reasons I attend church is to be taught the full meaning and understanding of the scriptures. I know in my heart that I love the Lord, and I pray that I am acceptable before His sight.

So, as I began to read and study the scriptures, I learned that Emmaus was a town near Jerusalem. The Bible says, "On the same day (of Christ's Resurrection) two men were going to a village called Emmaus, about seven miles from Jerusalem. They were talking with each other about everything that had happened. As they talked and discussed these things with each other, Jesus Himself came up and walked along with them; but they did not recognize Him.

He asked them, "What are you discussing together as you walk along?"

They stood still, their faces downcast. One of them, named Cleopas, asked Him, "Are you only a visitor to Jerusalem and do not know the things that have happened there in these days?"

"What things?" He asked.

"About Jesus of Nazareth," they replied. *"He was a prophet powerful in word and deed before God and all the people. The chief priests and our rulers handed Him over to be sentenced to death, and they crucified Him; but we had hoped that He was the one who was going to redeem Israel. And what is more, it is the third day since all this took place. In addition, some of our women amazed us.*

They went to the tomb early this morning but didn't find His body. They came and told us that they had seen a vision of angels, who said He was alive. Then some of our companions went to the tomb and found it just as the women had said, but Him they did not see."

He said to them, "How foolish you are, and how slow of heart to believe all that the prophets have spoken! Did not the Christ have to suffer these things and then enter His glory?" And beginning with Moses and all the prophets, He explained to them what was said in all the scriptures concerning Himself.

As they approached the village to which they were going, Jesus acted as if He were going farther. But they urged Him strongly, "Stay with us, for it is nearly evening; the day is almost over." So, He went in to stay with them.

Oh my God, was my first thought as I finished reading. The scriptures were starting to open up and come alive at that very moment. The revelation of it all started to take place as I pondered back on the scriptures.

When He was at the table with them, He took bread, gave thanks, broke it and began to give it to them. Then their eyes were opened, and they recognized Him, *and He disappeared from their sight. They asked each other, "Were not our hearts burning within us while He talked with us on the road and opened the scriptures to us?"*

They got up and returned at once to Jerusalem. There they found the Eleven and those with them assembled together and saying, "It is true! The Lord has risen and has appeared to Simon." Then the two told what had happened on the way and how Jesus was recognized by them when He broke the bread.

Oh my God, was my first thought as I finished reading. The scriptures were starting to open up and come alive at that very moment. The revelation of it all started to take place as I pondered back on the scriptures. The two men were on a journey to Emmaus when Jesus showed up in their lives. And although they didn't recognize Him at that point, Jesus ministered to them and reminded them of the prophecy spoken by the prophets and Himself. He broke bread with them and revealed Himself to them so they would fully believe, without doubt. As I thought about what I had read, I suddenly heard the voice again: "I want to do the same thing for you, Elgie. When you take your Emmaus Walk, I will show up and meet you there."

My spirit leaped inside with joy, and I began to communicate with the Spirit of God. "Me, Lord? You will show up on my Emmaus Walk and meet me there?"

"Yes!"

You know what? I didn't know if this revelation was true or not, but at that moment I started to believe it, claim it,

<footer>- 43 -</footer>

speak on it as if it was just a matter of time before it happened. Next, I told my husband, then I began to pray on it.

The following Wednesday at the Booster Service I gave a testimony at the church and began to tell them as well. But suddenly before I could even finish my testimony, Grace (another intercessory prayer partner), jumped up and shouted, "It's you, it's you!"

I didn't know what she was talking about, but she continued, "The Spirit has been speaking to me about sponsoring someone on their Emmaus Walk. I thought it was my friend at work, but when I approached her with the idea she said, 'Girl, the Lord has not spoken to me about an Emmaus Walk. I'm looking forward to it, but He has not spoken to me about that yet.'" Grace continued, "I thought she was just blowing me off, but listening to your testimony (and she turned from the congregation and looked back at me), it's you the Lord wants me to sponsor. I'll be your sponsor."

I could have fallen to the floor. God had prepared a "ram in the bush." I was so excited, and the church was on fire in the spirit, on one accord, shouting, "Amen...thank you, Jesus."

This was really contrary to what the enemy (working in my mind) wanted me to think or believe. But God is so good and I felt so grateful that I couldn't help but praise Him. The Bible says in James 4:7, "Submit yourselves, then, to God. Resist the devil, and he will flee from you." And in Matthew 21:21, Jesus said, "I tell you the truth, if you have faith and do not doubt, not only can you do what was done to the fig tree, but also you can say to this mountain, 'Go throw yourself into the sea,' and it will be done." So I just kept praising God for what could be.

REFLECTIONS

_____

_____

_____

_____

_____

_____

_____

_____

_____

_____

_____

_____

_____

_____

_____

_____

_____

_____

_____

Chapter Three

Faith, Trust, Obedience & Joy

Well, the church reviewed my application. I spoke with Rev. Wright and Rev. Lee, and they both were in agreement that I should take my walk at this time with the church approval. And as Grace said, she sponsored me as well as mailed my application off to the local Emmaus Community for registration. I felt as though I was on my way.

After a week went by, I started to check the mailbox every day looking for a

God is constantly pleading with me to trust Him always, in everything, and to never give up. But with all my faith, I still have a hard time trusting.

letter or something that would confirm my acceptance, but nothing came. And like I always do, I started to doubt that it would happen and blamed myself, wondering if I was getting a "big head."

God is constantly pleading with me to trust Him always, in everything, and to never give up. But with all my faith, I still have a hard time trusting. Can you have faith without trust, surely not, because with

God, they go hand in hand? I know I don't trust man any farther than I can see him. But I need to trust God; it's a vital step in my salvation.

Days went by, so I started to take my mind off the "Walk" to concentrate on other things I had to attend to such as the Prayer Summit. The committee had been meeting to organize the program, go over all the details, and prepare for signup and registration.

I wasn't even thinking about the Emmaus Walk when I got a letter in the mail dated March 7, 2003, stating, "CONGRATULATIONS! You have been accepted for the 'Walk to Emmaus' named in the box above! This 'Walk' will be held at Lake Sharon Retreat Center, Swisher Road, Lewisville, TX and here's what you need to bring."

I was so excited, I literally jumped for joy. I called my husband to tell him the good news and began thanking God in prayer.

A couple of days later Grace called to say she received her copy of the letter (as all sponsors do) and she began by saying, "Hello, Elgie, how are you feeling today? I received my letter from the Emmaus Community."

"Yes, I have, too, and God is so faithful," I answered.

"That is so true. And I'm sorry we didn't get the dates we were hoping for, but please forgive me, because I won't be able to attend the June 19th Walk, because my husband and I are attending the Marriage Retreat. But I will make sure you have another spon...."

Before she could complete her sentence, I interrupted, "Grace, I received my letter confirming my Walk in April, not June."

"No, Elgie, the letter was stating there was a waiting list for Walk #168, because it was already full, and they confirmed with us Walk #170 for June."

"No, Grace, I'm sure my letter read 'Walk #168' for April."

"Well, I don't have my letter with me to confirm," she said, "But I'll look at it again when I get home to be sure. But just in case, I'll start praying that it was for April," Grace very sweetly continued before saying good-bye and hanging up the phone.

I was so sure of my letter and the dates that I didn't bother to check right then. But when I did check two days later, there it was in large print: LOCAL WALK #170 dated for June 19th through June 22nd. I felt like "a heel," or more accurately an ostrich, because I wanted to "bury my head in the ground." Then I thought, "Oh no, I have to call Grace back and apologize. How foolish I was acting." I called Grace right away.

But when I got off the phone I was still devastated. I went to God in prayer through the Spirit and said, "Lord, You said I could go on the first Walk.

"Hello, Grace, its Elgie. I went back and read my letter more carefully, and I apologize for the mix-up. You were right; the confirmation was for June 19th. I'm so sorry I wasn't more receptive to what you were trying to tell me."

"No, don't worry about that. You were excited about the letter, and that's understandable."

"Yes, but I need to pay more attention to what I'm reading. Thanks again for being understanding, but I tell you the truth, Grace, I am not accepting the June date. God said I could go in April, and that's what I'm claiming."

"Now, that's the kind of faith I believe in," Grace answered, assuringly.

"I'm serious, I'm going to start praying, fasting and praying some more so I can go in April. I'm claiming that June will be better for someone else, and an April spot will come open for me."

"Very good, then we'll be in agreement together."

Grace also shared some testimonies about herself and her sister, which were wonderful words of encouragement to me.

But when I got off the phone I was still devastated. I went to God in prayer through the Spirit and said, "Lord, You said I could go on the *first* Walk. I testified at the Church, and now the Local Emmaus Community is saying that they have no available spots in April. Oh Lord, please help me, because I don't want to stand before Your people and say that You spoke to me and my speaking be in vain. Please help me, Lord."

Then it occurred to me...Satan. The enemy would have it to be this way, but "I

I was still claiming that the Lord said He would meet me there, and if the Lord said it, He cannot lie. So I continued to believe in my heart that God would open a door, praying and pleading with Him that He would not let me down.

rebuke you, Satan. You will not have dominion over my life." I spoke it out loud and clear from my mouth. "My Jesus said I could go in April, and that's what I'm counting on." Satan wants me to doubt God, but God said His Word will not come back void but will go out and accomplish everything it says it will do.

Even as I was praying this in my Spirit, my physical body was feeling defeated, shameful and let down. Where is my faith? I continued to ask myself out loud, "Where is my faith, my trust in God?"

I did eventually go back to the church to let them know that the letter said June, but I was still claiming April (in the name of Jesus). I called up my prayer partner, Sheila Dickerson, and she came in agreement with me (the Bible says where there are two or three gathered in my name, I shall be in the midst), and we were standing on His promises.

I was still claiming that the Lord said He would meet me there, and if the Lord said it, He cannot lie. So I continued to believe in my heart that God would open a door, praying and pleading with Him that He would not let me down.

Again, I had to take my mind off of this situation and get on with other things. I had to turn it over to God. It was drawing near to the date of the Prayer Summit, and I was at home working on the registration forms compiling the names in alphabetical order, separating them by paid and unpaid, and lunch or no lunch. Then I heard the voice again say, "Elgie," always softly but clearly. "At the Prayer Summit meeting Thursday night, the 27th, while you and the group are stuffing the bags and getting the name badges together, I want you to pass out a tea light candle to everyone and ask them to burn it in unity when they go home that night. This is what I want you to tell them: Place the burning candle somewhere in their home that night. Whenever they pass by the candle, stop and pray. Pray for the Summit, our

Pastor, the church, our guests, the nation, the schools, your family, your health, your finances, just anything or anyone you want God to bless -- just take a few minutes and pray, standing on the scripture, 1 Peter 2:24. He said, by doing this, we will be praying in unity, one with another, according to the Word of God in Matthew 18:20, *"For where two or three come together in my name, there I shall be in the midst."*

The voice said, "Inject the Light.
God is light – the Light outshines the darkness.
The fire will burn out – like the Blood of Jesus who purifies us.
The warmth of the fire – is like the Holy Spirit, which comforts us.
Do this for me. Tell the people."

And that night I wrote down (while listening) all that the voice told me to say and do. I dated it 3-27-03, the night I should do it, and I was determined to trust that the Lord was speaking to me and wanted to use me. No doubt this time; I praised him in body and spirit based on the scripture, Revelation 4:11.

"Yes, Lord, I will." I repeated in my mind, as I was "caught up in the Spirit" with awe at what the Lord was revealing to me.

And that night I wrote down (while listening) all that the voice told me to say and do. I dated it 3-27-03, the night I should do it, and I was determined to trust that the Lord was speaking to me and wanted to use me. No doubt this time; I praised him in body and spirit based on the scripture, Revelation 4:11.

Two days later, Cheryl (another prayer partner) called me on the phone, and we were discussing the Prayer Summit when I shared with her what the Spirit had put on my heart to do with the tea light candles, and she thought it was a wonderful idea. I went out and bought the candles.

The night of the 27th, the committee members were all there, working and getting things together. The voice spoke again, "Are you going to do what I asked you to do?" And again, I began to sweat and feel nervous. As I communicated in the Spirit, I began by saying, "Lord, I don't think anyone wants to hear that from me. I don't think people will be receptive to what you want me to do, and I'm too nervous." The Spirit asked me about three times more. Upon my last excuse, the Spirit left and I didn't feel close to God the rest of that time.

We had finished preparing all the bags and the name badges. We cleaned up and were starting to say our closing prayer to leave when Cheryl looked over and asked me, "Elgie, are you still going to do what you told me about the candles?" And she began to tell the group what I had shared with her.

I could feel the enemy pulling me back and also speaking in my mind saying, "No one wants to hear that, and don't do it." I tried to speak, but for a split second

> *While driving home, my spirit was renewed and I was so happy. I was glad that Cheryl had spoken up for me, for through her, God's request was carried out.*

no words would come forth. I was nervous, but then the Spirit broke loose and started talking, telling everyone what the Lord had revealed to me. I wasn't even sure what I was saying, but the words flowed out with ease. The Spirit of God was truly with me!

To my amazement and joy, everyone was receptive and wanted to have a part in it. As a result of my hesitance and disobedience, some people had already left for the night. But those who were still there all took a candle and said they would pray.

While driving home, my spirit was renewed and I was so happy. I was glad that Cheryl had spoken up for me, for through her, God's request was carried out. However, I kept apologizing to God, thanking Him for Cheryl, and questioning myself for allowing doubt to hold me back and consume me. For I know God's blessing was not about me or because of me, but God wants to know if I will obey Him, trust Him, and serve Him.

When I returned home that night I shared with Van what happened at church. I had not had a chance to look through the mail all day, so I did that while talking to Van. In the midst of this daily and mundane activity, I came upon a letter from the Local Emmaus Community. I hurried to open it with great anticipation. It was dated March 26, 2003, and the letter was congratulating me for being accepted for Walk #168 scheduled for April 24th through the 27th, and I had 10 days to respond. I screamed with joy!

The next day as the Prayer Summit kicked off, I was rejoicing with great joy for what God had done for me. He did not let me down, but made it possible for me to attend the Local Emmaus Walk on the dates He had revealed. Oh, how great God is!

That Saturday was very powerful at the Prayer Summit. The Lord blessed me and used me. And when Pastor Suzette Caldwell laid hands on me, I remember being "slain" and stretched out in the Spirit on the floor. I had no control, but I could hear myself praising the Lord, telling Him how faithful He is and how much I loved Him.

That night all who were present, Hamilton Park church members, guests and visitors, received a blessing. And we, the intercessory prayer team, got to see God's manifestation of the Spirit and the results of answered prayers.

REFLECTIONS

_____

_____

_____

_____

_____

_____

_____

_____

_____

_____

_____

_____

_____

_____

_____

_____

_____

_____

Chapter Four

Agape Love

As time approached closer to the dates of my scheduled Emmaus Walk, I began to feel a strong connection to God, and I would praise Him in my home daily. When I read my Bible, it seemed as though the words would jump off the page into my heart and set it on fire with joy. Sometimes streams of tears would just flow down my cheeks as I shouted, "Thank you, Jesus."

Around 2am one late night during "Holy Week," I was still awake and flipping through channels on TV hoping to find something good to watch when I ran across the "BET Easter Gospel Festival." It was featuring a lot of good Gospel singers, so I decided to watch it. But it was so good that I couldn't just watch it; I got up out of bed, found a blank videotape and was inspired to record it. And I'm so glad I did, because following that program some spiritual videos came on, and Jesus blessed me with two inspiring songs: "Shake Yourself Loose" by Vickie Winans and "Personal Jesus" by Tonex. I would play them over and over, and they would fill my spirit with joy as I sang and danced around the room. It was me and Jesus (in the Spirit) dancing, singing and having a good time. It felt good and I felt safe. I didn't care if my family or anybody else saw me or if they thought I was crazy or if they just didn't understand my praise. I just praised Him for what I knew and prayed for the day that they, too, would experience the true joy of God.

Well, April 24th finally arrived and I was excited and nervous at the same time. I was instructed in my Emmaus Walk letter to wear casual and comfortable clothing, and the most important thing was no cell phones, watches or outside interruptions for the entire three days.

Having a full 72-hour period set apart and devoted to God was an important aspect of the Walk to Emmaus. I was even instructed not to drive; my sponsor was responsible for getting me to and from the site. I didn't really know what to expect or what would take place in those three days, but I was ready.

I had never been camping and didn't spend the night away from home very often as a kid, so even at age 41, I was still nervous and kind of scared for Grace to leave me with people I didn't know.

Grace arrived at my house around 4:30 p.m., and we fellowshipped a bit before praying and going over my list to assure I had packed all that I would need. As we loaded the car, I could not help but notice and smell something delicious wrapped very carefully in the back seat. I thought to myself, what a wonderful wife and mother she is to plan a special dinner for her family even though she would be late getting home? Only special moms and wives do those types of things, and truly Grace is that type of woman. While riding, I kept thinking of how good that food smelled, and I wanted some so bad; I could just taste it. But the sweet conversation soon took my mind off of it, and we were headed to the campsite.

As we pulled into the entrance of the campsite, my heart began to rapidly speed up, and my hands became sweaty. I had never been camping and didn't spend the night away from home very often as a kid, so even at age 41, I was still nervous and kind of scared for Grace to leave me with people I didn't know. But I knew I had to quickly regain myself so she wouldn't see this fear on my face or hear it in my voice. Then immediately the scripture, Romans

8:31 dropped into my mind: "If God is for us, who can be against us?" Then suddenly my spirit was calmed with great confidence.

We unloaded the car and took in my bags. A lady was there to register me and provide me with a room number. I couldn't help but notice her sweet disposition as she pointed out where my room was and handed me a name badge. As I walked over to the room, I noticed my name on the door. The lady quickly pointed out a table in the corner full of additional toiletries such as toothpaste, toothbrush, soap, lotion, mints and many other things you could use if you ran out or just forgot to pack them. Wow, was my next thought as I turned to Grace and said, "I'm so glad I came!"

"Girl, you haven't seen anything yet. You are in for such a great blessing; this is just the beginning of what God has planned for you. Let me help you make your bed so you won't have to do that later," she continued speaking with love and concern. I unpacked some things, and I could feel a special bond building between Grace and me, and I felt proud that she was my sponsor.

After we finished, we drove across the lot to a large fellowship room where everyone was gathering for introduction and fellowship. As we got out of the car, I noticed Grace taking the food out of the back seat. And as she closed the door and started to walk toward the building, my wildest thought was, did she actually bring this food for us to eat tonight?

I wanted some of that food so badly ever since I smelled it earlier. It wasn't that I was hungry; it just smelled so good. So, I wondered if God would actually bless me to get some, and before I could even finish my thoughts, we were walking into the building where against the wall in the far left corner were tables and tables lined up together full of all types of foods. There were meats, vegetables, fruits, bread, desserts, drinks; you name it and it was there. And greater than that, Grace was adding her dish to the table! I could have fallen to the floor. God is so good! I stomped my foot and shook my head in amazement as my thoughts reminded myself of how God provides me with the desires of my heart, even in the small things, and at times when I don't even deserve them. I felt like I had entered the

Garden of Eden. The food was plentiful and I felt blessed.

After eating and fellowshipping, our names were called out in appreciation of being there. Then we lined up, said good-bye to our sponsors, and the journey began.

I then (in my mind) allowed doubt to settle in, and I began to question God again, "Are You sure You wanted me to come here, God? Maybe You did get me mixed up with someone else? There are other people who are more dedicated and deserving than I. I have a past.

We took a short tour and ended up in another large conference room where we gathered together for prayer. We were assigned seating at tables that were representing women of the Bible, such as, Ruth, Esther, Mary, Anna, etc. While sitting there talking to the women at my table (Table of Anna), the enemy attacked my mind and began to remind me of how unworthy I was. Surely I had not done anything great to deserve to be sitting here, and with all my past sins and faults, God had probably gotten me mixed up with someone else.

I then (in my mind) allowed doubt to settle in, and I began to question God again, "Are You sure You wanted me to come here, God? Maybe You did get me mixed up with someone else? There are other people who are more dedicated and deserving than I. I have a past. What about the drugs and the drinking? I get angry with people and I've cursed. Lord, what about...." But before I could get out another thought, or even focused back on the women at the table, a voice said, "SILENCE." The instruction from the facilitator's voice continued, "You will be silent for the remainder of the night. You will not utter another word or sound," and my lips were shut tight as though someone had glued them together.

We then watched a film and were headed to a small chapel to pray when the voice spoke to me again, "Elgie, you are my child and I have called you to this place. I am not concerned about your past, what you've done, where you've been, your what-abouts or your what-ifs. I love you and I want you to experience my AGAPE LOVE."

I didn't understand exactly what the Spirit was saying to me at that time, but I did remember studying about God's Agape Love in my Spiritual Gifts class under Rev. Wright. We learned in the class that the word "Agape" means and describes God's unconditional love given to us through grace, free to all men who believe. But could Jesus actually love me enough to bring me into His presence and into a place of rest right here on Earth?

As we returned to our rooms to settle in for the night, I started to feel a divine sense of peace and calmness. As I laid in my bunk, I was reminded of the voice back in my kitchen when Jesus said that He would meet me here. At that time, I was totally convinced it was Jesus (in the

As the days passed, the Lord began to open my understanding of His Word and help me to begin to trust Him more, leaning not on my own understanding, but learning to acknowledge Him in all that I do, that He may direct my path.

Spirit) who had been speaking to me and guiding me all along. "I believe in You, Jesus," I started to pray and communicate in the Spirit. "I love You and I want to learn more about You. I pray that You fill my heart with Your joy and write Your words on my lips and seal them in my heart that I may retrieve them in a time of praise, encouragement or healing." I laid there praying and thanking God for what He had done for me and how blessed I felt at that moment to be a part of this Walk #168.

As the days passed, the Lord began to open my understanding of His Word and help me to begin to trust Him more, leaning not on my own understanding, but learning to acknowledge Him in all that I do, that He may direct my path.

While at the Emmaus Walk I made new friends. We studied the Word; we discussed God's purpose for our lives. And Jesus truly revealed to me that life here on earth is not all about me, but also about my fellowman and woman. People that I don't know and those I do know, all are special in God's eyes, and He wants us to be happy and have peace in Him and with one another while we wait **patiently** for His return.

Jesus wants us to share His Word through our testimonies. Tell someone what He has done for you and how He has brought you through your good times and bad. We should seek Him by reading His Word (the Bible), and He will open up a whole new understanding of His will in our lives.

Each day at the Emmaus Walk brought a new beginning, a new revelation, and a new message. His Word was truly food for my soul just as meat and bread are food for my body. As I feasted on His Word and fellowshipped with His people, my heart was filled with joy, and I felt restored and set free from the bondage of the enemy of which I was bound.

The final night was the "icing on the cake." As we finished our studies, prayed and sang songs. We all held hands and proceeded out the door to return to our rooms for the night. But instead, the instructor took a different turn, and before I knew it; we were walking toward a line of people (all holding lighted candles), smiling with joy and waiting to greet us.

My past no longer mattered, nor were my faults before me in memory. It was as though Jesus had washed me clean and I was precious in His sight. The whole campground felt sacred. In the chapel, in the dining room, walking along the lake during free time, or just sitting on the porch laughing with the pastors and other table members, no matter where I was or what I was doing, I could feel the Spirit of the Lord cuddling me. For once in my life, I felt accepted and at peace. I knew a time would return when the enemy would strike again, but for now, I was at peace with myself, and the world.

Thank You, Jesus! Thank You, Jesus! Thank You, thank You, thank You, was all I could say or think in my mind! Wow! "How great is His love," my lips kept repeating. And when I would turn to a table member or just see another person on the Walk, they, too, had a glow about them and were praising the Lord in Spirit and in Truth.

The final night was the "icing on the cake." As we finished our studies, prayed and sang songs. We all held hands and proceeded out the door to return to our rooms for the night. But instead, the instructor took a different turn, and before I knew it; we were walking toward a line of people (all holding lighted candles), smiling with joy and waiting to greet us.

We walked through the line and into a dark room lit by candlelight, and the room was filled with people of all races, genders, sizes and heights. All of their faces were filled with joy, and there was a glow about them that far outshined the light from the lighted candles. You could see the joy on their faces and feel the love from their hearts.

Some of the people I knew, and others I didn't. But it didn't matter, they all were there for one purpose, to praise God and show love to His people. Again, my heart was filled with amazement, and I was left speechless.

When Sunday, the last day of the Walk, approached, all the women there were renewed, restored, encouraged, uplifted, healed, transformed and made over. And, once again, Jesus blessed me with a desire of my heart by rewarding me with a beautiful, beautiful, rainbow-colored crochet necklace with a cross hanging on it that said, "Christ is Counting On You."

On me....He's counting on me, I thought as I admired the necklace. All the leaders wore one throughout the Walk, and I wanted one so badly. And now

Jesus had placed one on my neck and is counting on me to share His Word.

I **must** **do** **something**! This was my entire thought as we finished our last prayer, said our good-byes as I looked out the car window while driving away. I felt as though I was entering back into civilization again. Like I had been away, taken up, separated, cut off from the world, and now I was back.

What would I do?

Who would I tell?

Would they believe me?

I MUST DO SOMETHING!

Contact Elgie

ElgieLoyd@yahoo.com

www.ingramcontent.com/pod-product-compliance
Lightning Source LLC
Chambersburg PA
CBHW071102090426
42737CB00013B/2433